BUCK
THE POPEYED CROW

by

Helen Williamson

Illustrated

by

Efe Peters

From the Miss Shai Shai series

Buck the Pop Eyed Crow

Williams and King Publishers

Orlando, Florida

ISBN 9780999840610

Printed in the United States of America.

BUCK
THE POPEYED CROW

Leary

Monica

Mondrea

Miss Angel

Buck

Pearl

Lack

HELEN WILLIAMSON
ILLUSTRATED BY EFE PETERS

B uck is looking for Lack will he find him?

It was early one spring morning, Buck the Pop-Eyed Crow was sitting on the back on the picket fence like he had done many times before. But there was something different about this time.

He thought to himself, there was something different about this morning, then he began to cry. He was overwhelmed with the memories of Lack. He began to talk to himself:

"I sit on the back of this fence everyday and watch the birds flying through the sky. As I watch the birds fly I always think of Lack. I dream about him when I am asleep and I cry for him when I am awake. I wonder everyday where he may be or what he might be doing. I love Lack and I want to see him or at least hear that he is alright."

Buck began thinking and wondering, what will I do? It has been a long time since I've seen Lack and the only way I will ever see him again is to go and find him.

"Now I know what I must do! I must go and find Lack!" he yelled. "I have no idea where to start looking for him. I might as well start right here behind this fence. I will go to the east and I will take a shortcut through the ginger apple field. I am not a stranger to the ginger apple field. They don't like strangers in their ginger apple field. Lack and I use to play in the field. But that was a long time ago.

"I still remember when Lack and I would run through this field and hide from the buzzards and crows. Sometimes we would hide inside the ginger apple field, and sometimes we would hide under the ginger apple trees. We were always hiding somewhere in this field. Hiding was a way of life for us back then. Lack and I were always bullied because we looked different from the other crows and buzzards.

"I am a pop-eyed crow with two big feet and Lack is a teeny, tiny little buzzard with no feet. We were different for sure. The other crows would say to me everyday 'Buck, Buck the Pop-Eyed crow where did you get those eyes? I would start crying and the crows and buzzards would start laughing. Then the crows would say, 'Keep the big feet they look comfortable, but get rid of those pop-out, pop-eyes' and they would laugh more and the more. The more I cried the louder they laughed. They laughed so hard that they would start crying. When the laughter stopped, the bullying would start.

"They kicked Lack and I, then threw ginger apples at us. The crows would stop bullying us for a few minutes so that the buzzards could start to bully us. Those buzzards were so mean they would pull Lack's feathers and throw sand in his face, then laugh. The crows and buzzards thought the things they were doing to us were funny. But Lack and I were not laughing and we were always scared in the ginger apple field. Bullying is never funny.

"Well here I am in the middle of the ginger apple field and I don't know what to do. I am hoping I will come across a person or a animal that may have seen Lack recently. He is well known around the Buzzard Tribe.

"Oh, I am sorry I'm doing all this talking and you don't know my friend Lack. Do you? Lack is my teeny, tiny, little brother. He is a buzzard and a special one for sure. He is smaller than the average buzzard, that's how he got the name Teeney Tiny. He's my brother and my friend.

"Lack and I are different from the other crows and buzzards, we are special. The other buzzards and crows thought we were different and we are. What they didn't know, and what we didn't know at that time is, being different is not a bad thing but a good thing - it makes you special. Look at me, I am the only pop-eyed crow with two big feet in the whole wide world. If you don't believe it look around in the whole world and see for yourself. I am the only one and that's what makes me special. My pop-eyes and my big feet make me different and being different also makes me special."

Buck smiled and mumbled to himself, "Lack is special too. There is not another teeny, tiny, little buzzard with no feet anywhere in this world! Lack is the only one and that makes him special."

Buck smiled again and thought to himself, I can't be bullied anymore I know now that I am a special crow. I am a one of a kind of crow and I have value. No crow or buzzard can ever bully me again. I know now who I am and knowing who you are is a giant step in life. My mother and father are normal but I am different. I was born a pop-eyed crow with two big feet.

It was difficult for Lack too because it was hard enough being a pop-eyed crow with big feet, but having a brother with no feet made it even harder for me. It was hard for Lack having a pop-eyed crow with two big feet for a brother. Those were hard times for us. We were always bullied everywhere we went, and sometimes we were hit and kicked. We were always laughed at and made to be afraid. But those years are past and gone. We got through those years with our feathers attached. We are not together anymore and I miss him everyday. Mom, the Crow and Pop the Buzzard flew north. My teeny, tiny, little brother flew south, and I flew west and ended up at a place in Blueberry, U.S.A. called Sammy's Zoo. That is where I have been all these years until I decided to move back here to the ginger apple field.

As Buck was thinking and wondered what he would do next, his mind went back to the talk he had with his friend, Pearl the white beaver. He remembered telling her how much he missed Lack. He remembered her saying to him, "Buck, Buck, my friend if you miss Lack so much you must do something about it."

"Something like what?" I asked Pearl.

"You must go and find Lack," she answered.

Buck thought to himself, if I am already in the middle of the ginger apple field, I might as well start my search right here.

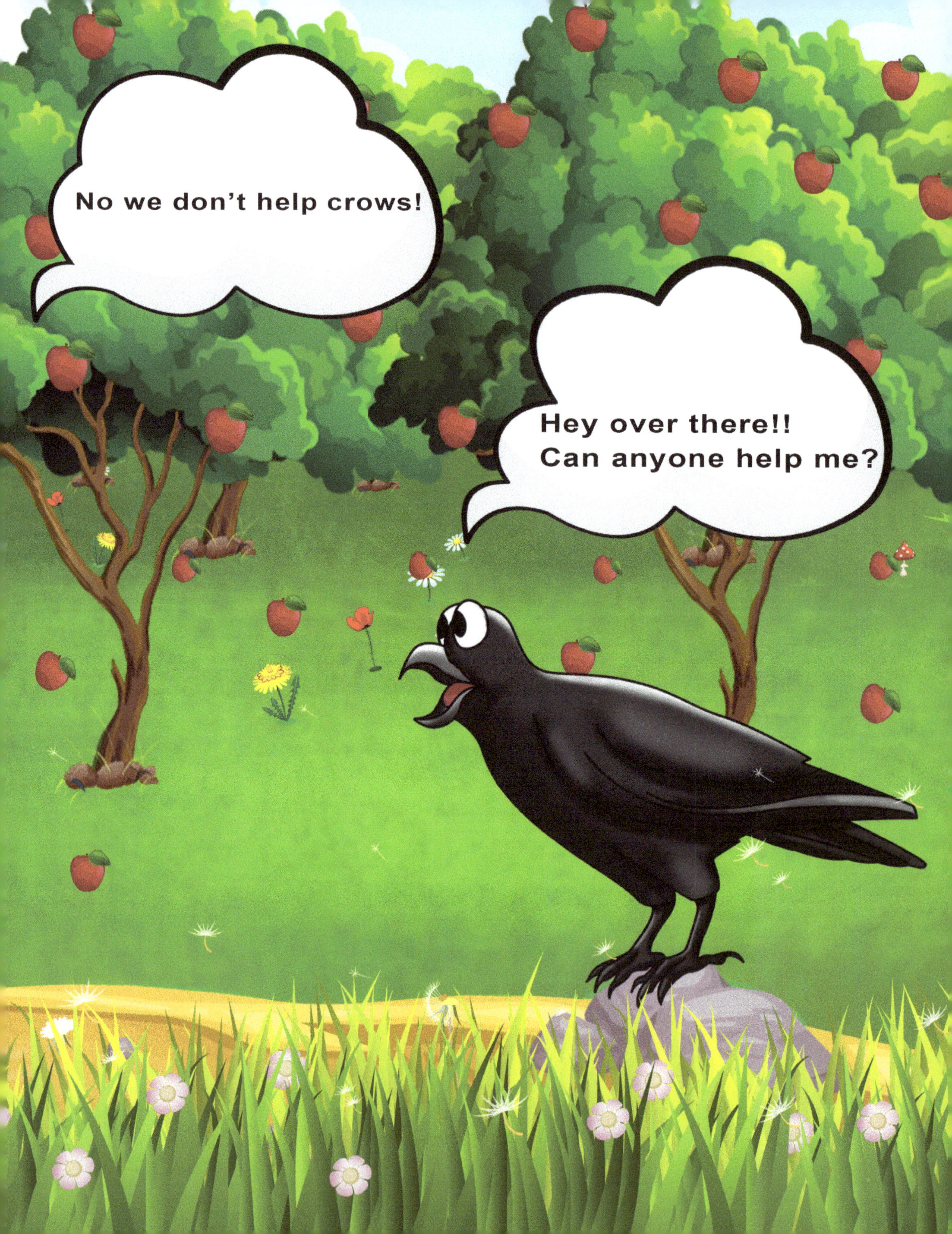
No we don’t help crows!
Hey over there!! Can anyone help me?

Buck was scared and shaking more than a worm on a fishing pole. Now that's shaking!!

"What must I do?" he asked himself. "I would call out to someone but I don't see or hear a person or creature stirring. It is as quiet as a mouse and I am scared. Now I am shaking even faster than a worm on a fishing pole. But I must find Lack. I will not end my search until I find him."

He started to look between the ginger apple trees.

"Hey, over there can anyone hear me?" he yelled out.

"I am Buck the Pop-Eyed Crow and I am looking for Lack. Can someone, anyone help me? I need some help. I am looking for my teeny, tiny, little brother. He's a buzzard. I have not seen him in so many years and I have missed him a lot and I want to see him. Will someone please help? Hey, over there can you help me?"

"No!" said a voice coming from under the third ginger apple tree. "We don't help crows especially pop-eyed ones. We don't like them, so go home crow. Pop-Eyed Crow go home! We don't know any buzzards at all, so go home crow. We don't know Lack, never heard of him, so go home crow!"

"But listen to me." Buck said to the voice that was coming from under the third ginger apple tree. "If I tell you a little bit about him you might remember seeing him somewhere or sometime in the past."

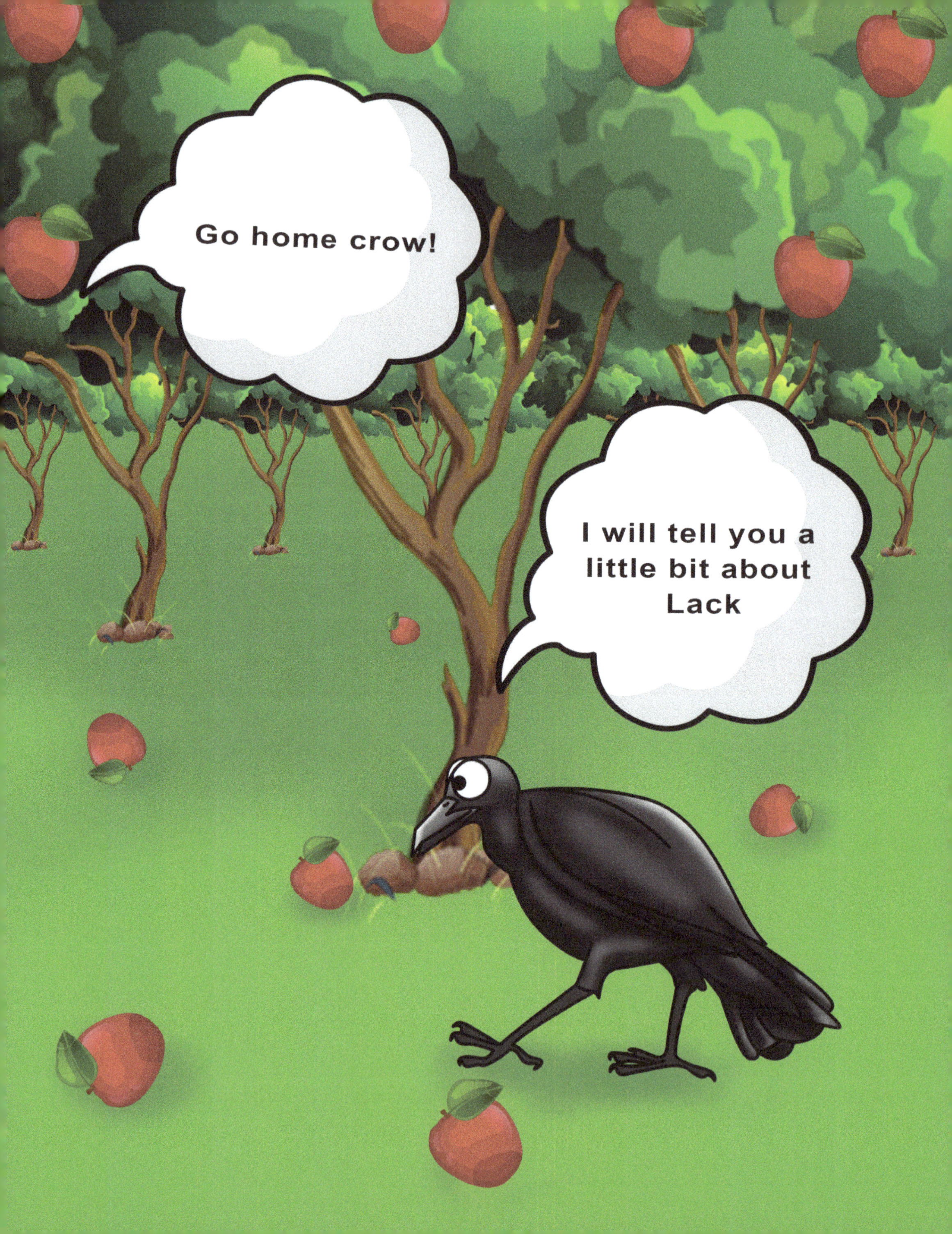
Go home crow!
I will tell you a little bit about Lack

"Don't bother telling me anything about anyone because I don't remember anything. I forget about everything. If I saw him I already forgot.

So go home crow, you are not welcomed in our ginger apple field. So you go home now, crow. Do you hear me?" said the voice. "Go home crow!"

"Yes, I do hear you. I cannot go home I must find my teeny, tiny brother Lack and I do need some help."

"Well you ain't gonna get any help, so go home crow." repeated the voice.

"Listen crow!" the voice yelled. "Can't you see by now no one is going to help? Those eyes are big enough to see Mars from earth. So, look through those big pop-eyes and go back to where you come from and leave us alone crow!"

Buck thought to himself, everyone has a "stop-now" point, and this voice has caused me to reach my stop now point.

"Listen voice, whoever or whatever you are, I am Buck the Pop-Eyed Crow and I have had enough of your nasty and mean words so you can stop now! Talking is over! I will not go home. I will find Lack with or without your help. Now do you hear, me Voice?"

Moments later, a very soft and lovely voice spoke out and said, "I am sorry Crow. If my brother were missing I would want someone to help me find him. Now tell me what can I do to help you find Lack? My name is not Voice. Everyone calls me Leary the Bully, and I am a little bit of a bully, but you know that by now. Everyone in this ginger apple field is afraid of me. Why are you not afraid of me?" asked Leary.

Listen voice, I am Buck the Pop- Eyed Crow
I am sorry crow. I am Leary, The Bully

"I am afraid of you, but I love Lack more than I am afraid of you. Love overpowers fear. You must understand, Lack and I have always been bullied. So bullying doesn't bother me anymore because I found a place where everyone is different and happy to be different. I will tell you about it later. I must go now and find Lack," Buck answered Leary.

Leary looked at Buck with a sad look on her face, she began to cry. "I have a question to ask you," Leary said.

"Okay, what's the question?" Buck asked.

"Once we find Lack and you go back to where you came from where everyone is different and happy to be different, will you take me back with you? I don't want to be a bully anymore," cried Leary in a calm voice.

Buck also began to cry and answered, "I would be happy if you came home with me, but first I must find Lack."

He began to call out to his brother, "Lack! Lack! can you hear me? Where are you?" No answer came.

"Hey over there, what's the fuss about?" Another voice asked.

"I am Buck the Pop-Eyed Crow, and Leary the Bully is with me. We are looking for Lack. Have you seen him?"

"You said you and Leary are looking for Lack? What the heck is a Lack?" the voice asked.

"Lack is a teeny, tiny, little buzzard with no feet. He's my brother." Buck answeed the voice which was coming from a distance.

"Did you say Lack is a teeny, tiny footless buzzard? How can that be? You are pop-eyed crow with big feet. How can your brother be a teeny, tiny, little buzzard with no feet?" asked the voice.

"I don't have time to explain I must find him. Will you help me?" Buck asked.

"Heck no! I can't leave this ginger apple field," said the voice. "I am Miss Angel, the ginger apple keeper. Every morning I shine all these ginger apples you see around you."

"I shine all the ginger apples every morning and if I leave the them alone they will get dull and I cannot let that happen, so I must not leave this field. But I do know someone that might be able to help you find your brother Lack."

"Who?" Buck asked.

"Monica. If anyone can help you it will be Monica."

"Who is Monica?"

"Monica is an ugly bat that lives in a clock under the last ginger apple tree. She's crazy."

Buck looked at Miss Angel again and asked, "How can I find the last ginger apple tree?"

Who are you guys?

"Leary the Bully can show you the way to Monica's clock. But let me warn you Buck she is crazy as a bed bug and noisy as an owl. But you will find that out soon enough. Goodbye and good luck Crow. You will need all the luck you can get and more," replied Miss Angel to Buck.

"Miss Angel is right. I know the way to Monica's clock. Come follow me, and I will show you the way. But remember what Miss Angel said - that she is crazy! I know her well. We use to eat ginger apples together. But I had to stop visiting her."

"Why?" asked Buck.

"She is crazy and she thinks everyone that comes through the ginger apple field is her silly sister Mondrea. You see Mondrea thought she was smart and she left Monica alone to go find a college in the big city. Mondrea could not find the college so she decided to go back home, now she cannot find her way back home. We are getting close to Monica's clock. If you look over there you will see the clock."

They walked for a few more minutes.

"We are here, there is Monica's clock and there's Monica eating fried ginger apple and jelly. Buck you must be patient we might be here for awhile. She likes to talk because she doesn't get many visitors. Plus she's crazy!"

When Leary was getting ready to say 'hello', Monica called out to them, "Hello boys!"

Buck laughed out loud and said, "We are not boys. I am Buck the Pop-Eyed Crow and Leary the Bully is with me."

"Oops! I'm sorry," said Monica. "You must excuse me. Without my glasses everyone looks like boys to me." She smiled and looked Buck into his eyes and asked, "Why are you and Leary the Bully here at my clock. This is my clock and the both of y'all are trespassing. Now get to stepping boys. You are not welcomed here at my clock. This is Monica's clock and I am Miss Monica!"

Leary whispered to Buck reminding him that Miss Angel already told him that Monica was a crazy bat. Buck had a serious look on his face as he looked Monica in her face and asked her, "Have you seen a teeny, tiny, little buzzard?"

"Who wants to know?" asked Monica.

"Me. I do. He is my brother, Lack." Monica kicked a rock on the ground and replied, "Crow, everyone is looking for someone. I'm looking for my silly sister Mondrea. She left three years ago to go to college and I have not seen her since. I know she cannot find her way home have you seen her?"

Buck and Leary look at each other, "No, we have not seen Mondrea," they both said at the same time.

"Well you have not seen Mondrea and I have not seen a teeny, tiny, buzzard. Now, how do you like them apples?" replied Monica.

Buck sat on the steps of Monica's clock and looked up toward the sky and began crying. He turned and said Leary and Monica, "I will never find Lack, will I?"

"If you stop crying, I will try to help you find Lack or at least point you in the right direction," said Monica. "Now if you go in that direction," she pointed, "and go across the fuzzy rug to the buzzard trail to the Buzzard River and ask some of the buzzards if they have seen Lack. They will know if he is there or has been there because all the buzzards hang out at the Buzzard River. Now that's all I can tell you Crow. It is getting close to my nap time and I am getting sleepy. You must go now. I hope you find Lack and I hope Mondrea finds her way home."

"Goodbye Crow and goodbye Bully."

"Goodbye," they all said at the same time and waved.

Buck and Leary were walking in the middle of the buzzard trail laughing and talking when Leary got hungry.

"Buck, Buck," she said. "I'm hungry."

Buck told Leary he was hungry and sleepy.

"I have some ginger apples in my pocket. I brought them from the ginger apple field. We can stop here under this big rock and eat these ginger apples and take a nap."

"Sounds like a good idea. Let's do it." Leary said.

Buck and Leary sat under the big rock and ate ginger apples that Buck had in his pocket. Leary was almost finished eating her last ginger apple when she heard a soft soothing sound coming from behind the rock. She looked and saw a river filled with buzzards swimming back and forth.

There were the other buzzards playing on the riverbank. Buck finished eating his ginger apple and by now was almost asleep.

"It's the Buzzard River! It must be!" She looked over the river hoping she would see Lack. After looking around the whole river twice she saw something amazing. It was a teeny, tiny, little buzzard with no feet talking to a sad looking bat that looked lost.

Leary said to herself, I wonder if that is Lack and Mondrea. I must tell Buck, she thought.

"Buck! Come now! Come quickly! You must see this!" she called out to him.

Buck stood straight up with a frightened look on his face as he woke up from a deep sleep. He was dreaming about dancing with angels.

"What's wrong?" he asked.

"Nothing is wrong. You must peep behind the rock, you're going to be amazed!" Leary exclaimed.

Buck peeped behind the rock. He was amazed! Just as Leary said. He saw a teeny, tiny, little buzzard with no feet talking to a sad and lost looking bat. The only words that could come from his mouth was, "It's Lack!!" he yelled. "It must be Lack! It must be. Who else could it be?"

"How can we be sure?" Leary asked him.

"It has got to be Lack!" Buck repeated excitedly. "How many teeny, tiny, little buzzards are there? I believe there is only one and the one is Lack! Let's go closer and call out his name. If he doesn't answer we will know that it's not him. If he does answer and it's Lack, I will be so happy!"

"I will be happy with you," replied Leary. "You must get ready to call him."

"Are you ready to call his name?"

"Yes, I'm ready!"

"Lack! Lack!!" Buck yelled.

The teeny tiny buzzard looked around and asked, "Who is calling my name?"

Buck was laughing and crying at the same time. "I am calling you. I am your brother Buck the Pop-Eyed Crow. I have missed you and I have been looking for you. I am so glad to see you today!"

Lack cried too, "I have missed you too. I am so glad to see you today."

Buck hugged Lack and asked him, "Who is this sad bat you have with you? She looks so unhappy."

"This is Mondrea," Lack answered. "She is sad because she needs help and I told her I would help her. Mondrea left the ginger apple field three years ago to go to college but she could not find the college so she came back to the ginger apple field to find her sister Monica and her clock. Buck, we really need to help her!"

Buck and Leary looked at each other and laughed very hard.

"What's so funny?" Lack asked Buck.

Leary walked up to Lack and looked him in both eyes, "We know where the clock is."

"We just left Monica's clock!" said Buck. "Isn't it funny how things happen? Monica helped me find you, and I am helping her sister to find her."

Leary started crying.

"What's wrong? asked Buck.

"Nothing is wrong, everything is good," said Leary. "I am so happy because you have found Lack, Mondrea will find Monica, and I have found all of y'all".

The End

A Word from Miss Shai-Shai

"Bullying is never fun and always hurtful."

Miss Shai-Shai

Other books in Miss Shai Shai series

Miss Shai Shai the Sunflower Princess

Sammy's Zoo

The Pitiful Kangaroo in the Strawberry
Pumpkin Patch

Coot the Peeping Snake

About the Author

Helen Williamson is originally from Columbus County, North Carolina and currently lives in the Central Florida area. Despite being widowed at an early age, very little education and in economic hardship she managed to successfully raise five children. Her eldest daughter passed from Lupus, so part of her charitable giving includes contributions to the Lupus Foundation with the hope that a cure will be found within her lifetime.

At the age of fifty, Helen decided to go back to school and earn her high school diploma. She is also active in her church and has a passion to write children's books, using them as teaching tools to encourage self-esteem and self-value in our younger generation.

www.ingramcontent.com/pod-product-compliance
Lightning Source LLC
Chambersburg PA
CBHW040256100426
42811CB00011B/1284